PENRITH

THROUGH TIME

Dr Bryan Lindley
& Dr Judith Heyworth

AMBERLEY PUBLISHING

About the Authors

Judith Heyworth studied Medicine at the University of Liverpool, has a Diploma in Public Health and is a Fellow of the Royal College of Radiologists. She worked around Liverpool and in London, before spending many years as a Consultant Radiologist in a South Manchester Teaching Hospital. After retirement, she spent nearly two years as a locum Consultant Radiologist at Cumberland Infirmary, Carlisle. Like her husband, Bryan, she has enjoyed photography since schooldays; they have both embraced digital photography with enthusiasm and have awards from the Photographic Alliance of Great Britain and Royal Photographic Society.

Bryan Lindley has a first-class Honours Degree and Doctorate in Engineering from University College London, of which he is a Fellow. He worked at director level for multinational engineering companies and completed his career as Chairman of a Cumbrian NHS Healthcare Trust covering community and mental health. He was awarded the CBE in 1982. Since schooldays he has had a great interest in photography and is a member of Penrith and District Camera Club, founding Penrith Contemporary Archives Group with his wife Judith. They live in Penrith in a house they designed and had built themselves, and are involved in many local activities. Bryan has a son and granddaughter.

First published 2013

Amberley Publishing
The Hill, Stroud, Gloucestershire, GL5 4EP
www.amberley-books.com

Copyright © Dr Bryan Lindley and Dr Judith Heyworth, 2013

The right of Dr Bryan Lindley and Dr Judith Heyworth to be identified as the Authors of this work has been asserted in accordance with the Copyrights, Designs and Patents Act 1988.

ISBN 978 1 4456 1274 4 (print)
ISBN 978 1 4456 1297 3 (ebook)

British Library Cataloguing in Publication Data.
A catalogue record for this book is available from the British Library.

Typesetting by Amberley Publishing.
Printed in Great Britain.

Introduction

Penrith is a small but characterful and historic market town in Cumbria. Man has inhabited the locality since prehistoric times, as evidenced by artefacts and stone circles. The Roman occupation around Penrith, then known as Epiacum, was significant through lead and silver mining. In Roman times, Penrith and the River Eamont crossing were at the confluence of major routes along High Street by Ullswater and on towards Carlisle and Hadrian's Wall. Little is known of the 'Dark Ages' although, as in many other places, there are links to King Arthur and the Knights of the Round Table. The area is also famous for the exploits of the Border Reivers from the late thirteenth to early seventeenth centuries. The Reivers were wild and fierce horsemen, well-armed in armour and chain mail, who despoiled the Border region, burning down the wooden habitations and taking cattle, possessions and people. In Penrith, evidence of the raids is provided by Penrith Castle, the late fourteenth-century pele tower at Hutton Hall, and the 'Yards' off many of the old streets. The latter have a narrow entrance that could be defended, leading to groups of dwellings and space for animals.

Following the accession of James I to the British throne, the Borders became less war-ridden, and Penrith emerged as a prosperous market town. Trade and agriculture boomed. There was a town-centre school attended by William Wordsworth, his sister and wife-to-be. Much of the character of the town was created in the Victorian era. Churches were established, including the beautiful St Andrew's, as well as Christ church (a second Anglican church), the Methodist church, Roman Catholic church, a Quaker Meeting House, and churches of other denominations. Robinson's School practised in an Elizabethan building which is now Penrith and Eden Museum. There are two designated Conservation Areas: around the town centre; and the 'New Streets', where locals had a rash of building houses along streets leading up Beacon Hill to the Beacon Edge Road, which skirts the hill on a more or less level contour, 200 feet above the town. There is a Beacon monument of 1719 at the top of the hill, marking the site where a beacon was fired to signal a Napoleonic invasion or threats from the north. The architecture is largely traditional Victorian, using local Lazonby dark red sandstone. Many garden and field boundaries are walled in this stone, and there are some fine Victorian houses. A Cottage Hospital was built on Beacon Edge, and next door was the cemetery. A rather grand Town Hall was created from two adjoining Adam-style houses, one owned by the Wordsworth family. Queen Elizabeth Grammar School flourished, followed later by Ullswater Community College.

The main stimulus in the mid-Victorian years was the coming of the railway. Goods and people became mobile, and tourism in the Lake District grew at a pace. People left trains at Penrith to head for Ullswater by horse-drawn coach or motor charabanc. Penrith is now at a junction of the main east–west A66 trunk road and the M6 motorway, while the West Coast Main Line railway through Penrith joins London with Glasgow and Edinburgh. The new M6 motorway bypassed Penrith, where the A6 trunk route through the town had been the main route to Scotland and caused great congestion through a very narrow section.

The Cattle Auction Mart was re-established west of the M6 junction 40, and the former Mart became the site for Safeway (later acquired acquired by Morrisons) and the thriving Penrith Players' Theatre. Penrith always prided itself on its many independent shops selling a wide variety of goods. Several have a very long history and attract the population of a large hinterland as well as tourists and other visitors. The Penrith Millennium Trail has eighty-three bronze plaques let into the pavement, marking a series of walks radiating from the town centre, illustrated leaflets conveying aspects of the town's history.

After years of discussion and consultation, Eden District Council allowed a large Sainsbury's supermarket to be built near the town centre on land originally donated by the Lowthers for recreational purposes. This has catalysed a rate of change in the built environment of Penrith unequalled since, in relative terms, that of mid-Victorian times. The key component became a major development known as the New Squares. Vast construction of new housing and apartments, affordable housing, more retail shops, new car parking, a move of the town football club out of town, a new fire station and many other new buildings, as well as Sainsbury's and Booths supermarkets, has led to widespread changes in appearance. The authors present a visual impression compared with the old town.

Acknowledgements

The authors would like to express their gratitude to the early photographers who recorded the town's history, some of whom assembled collections of images. We are especially indebted to: the *Cumberland and Westmorland Herald* for kind permission to include photographs while recognising retention of copyright; also Cranstons for photographs of their founder and the Cumbrian Food Hall; and Penrith Farmers & Kidd for photographs of the former Auction Mart and the Skirsgill Mart. We also gratefully appreciate the kindness of the following: Lawrence Marlow collection; Mike Best collection; Gordon Rigg collection; Frank Boyd collection; Gordon Browne collection; and Judith Clarke and Sydney Chapman of Penrith and Eden Museum for images in their care, and with formal permission from Eden District Council. Ken Twentyman and John Bowerbank kindly gave access to images in their possession. The authors are indebted to members of Penrith and District Camera Club who volunteered to record Penrith changing over the years 2008 to 2013 under the aegis of Penrith Contemporary Archives Group (a special interest group of the Camera Club) coordinated by the authors. Those volunteers are: Maureen Birkett, Helen Boyd, Gina Bracken, Irving Butterworth, Valerie Evans, Andrew Gosling, Mike Haythornthwaite, Judith Heyworth, Christine Hurford, Peter Koch-Osborne, Frank Kirkby, Bryan Lindley, Kevin Lodge, Joan Mark, Dave Mark, Jane Peet, Lisa Smith, Paul Swain, Iain Walker, and Jennifer Watson. All images, both historic and recent, are subject to the author's copyright, and may not be reproduced other than with written permission. All royalties from the sale of *Penrith through Time* go to the Camera Club. Recording five years' work, almost 3,000 images are lodged with Penrith and Eden Museum, adding to the club's exhibition material for the millennium year (also with the Museum).

Wordsworth House, *c.* 1900, and Town Hall, 2013

The Town Hall was converted from a pair of Adam-style houses dating from 1791. One of these was known as Wordsworth House, the residence of Captain John Wordsworth. He was a sea captain and died in 1819; a celebratory wall plaque is mounted on the façade. There was lively debate beyond Penrith about the Town Hall, it being argued that the architectural integrity and appeal of the original building would be lost. Canon Rawnsley, a co-founder of the National Trust, was successful in having the central staircase and some windows retained. On the façade of the completed Town Hall is a carved facsimile of the town seal incorporating the cross of St Andrew. The original brass seal (*see page 33*) was discovered in Brampton, possibly dropped by a Scots raider in the fourteenth century, and now in safekeeping at Penrith and Eden Museum.

South African War Memorial, 1906 and 1999
Known locally as the 'Black Angel' but intended to depict the 'Angel of Peace crowning the Heroes', the memorial to the Boer War of 1899–1902 was unveiled by Brigadier-General Rimington in 1906. The bronze figure was a reproduction of that chosen by two other towns for the same purpose, saving money for the War Memorial Committee. It was originally in Corney Square near the Town Hall, where the young girl seems to have had a bevy of admirers! In 1964, the memorial was moved to Castle Park because it was felt that the fumes and pollution from the congested A6 traffic close by were damaging the statue.

Musgrave Monument, 1920s and 2013

The Musgrave monument and clock tower stands proudly in the Market Square of Penrith, creating an iconic image for the town. It was erected in 1861 by public subscription, as a tribute to Sir George and Lady Musgrave on the death in Madrid of their son, Philip, at the age of twenty-six. Sir George was the local Member of Parliament, and the family much lauded in the town. The railings have been removed and four new traditional standard lights erected around the periphery. The monument has its own 'traffic island' decorated by newly-installed planters.

Devonshire Arcade, 1912 and 2012

An archway off Market Square (partly Devonshire Street) leads to the Devonshire Arcade. The spacious hall had stalls for fresh fruit and vegetables, eggs, butter and other dairy produce, as well as live poultry. Concerts, lectures and election meetings were held within its walls. It was redeveloped in 1991 and now contains a variety of shops, retaining an area devoted to food outlets including two restaurants, a baker, butchers and fresh fish. Above is now the location of the excellent and popular Penrith Library, operated by Cumbria County Council. The former Grammar School building from 1857 was incorporated into the library.

St Andrew's Church, 1900 and 2012

Ancient religious origins were already known when the site was given to the Bishop of Carlisle in 1133. The present church was rebuilt in 1720–22, incorporating a medieval west tower. The interior is well-proportioned and rather grand. The architect is believed to have been Nicolas Hawksmoor. Two brass chandeliers in the nave were given by the Duke of Portland to the people of Penrith for their loyalty during the Jacobite rising of 1745. Mural paintings in the chancel are by the Penrith-born artist Jacob Thompson.

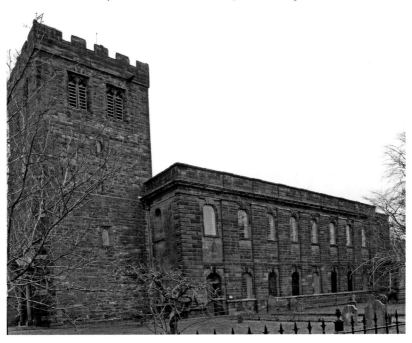

Giant's Grave, *c.* 1900 and 2013

The intriguing Giant's Grave in St Andrew's churchyard is surrounded by conflicting history and mythology. It consists of two badly weathered cross shafts and four Norse 'hogback' tombstones dating from the tenth century. It may mark the burial place of Owen, King of Cumbria from AD 920 to 937. Alternatively, some think buried there is Sir Owen Caesarius, who dwelt in the Giant's Cave on the banks of the River Eamont near Penrith. The grave was reputedly opened in the sixteenth century, finding 'the great long shank bones and other bones of a man, and a broadsword'.

St Andrew's Place,
c. 1950 and 2012

The walk around St Andrew's churchyard, here looking towards Market Square, is full of interest from the variety of buildings and uses. One finds the Tudor house, an example of the earliest domestic architecture in Penrith, indeed the oldest dated house, with the inscription 'RB 1563'; the owner is believed to have been Roger Bertram. Later, it became Dame Birkett's School, where among its pupils in 1776 was the future poet William Wordsworth, his sister Dorothy and his prospective wife Mary Hutchinson. The poet's forbears and relatives were more closely associated with Penrith and its surrounding district than is generally appreciated.

Changing Uses of Shops, 2013

Many shops in the town have closed, now offering services rather than goods. There is a plethora of hairdressers, beauty salons and nail bars, as well as estate agents, travel agents, building societies and charity shops. Here, we see one of three tattooists, others also offering body piercing, which have opened in the past two years. Often there is minimal revamp of the premises, but they open during hours to suit their clients.

Graham's, 1900 and 2013

James and John Graham groceries and delicatessen has traded in this imposing and historic building (to the right of the monument) overlooking Market Square since 1880, having been established in 1793. The high building to the left of the monument is now Barclays Bank; that to the right with the tower feature was Goldsmith's (part of the earlier Angel Square development) which has now closed. Recently, we see the Farmer's Market with one stall taken by Graham's, offering samples to entice people into the shop.

Thompson's, *c.* 1900, and HSBC Bank, 2013

Thompson's was a vast establishment in its day, carrying a huge variety of ironmongery goods and even possessing the skills and workshops to make many of its wares. In 1908, Henry Thompson moved to Castlegate from Market Square and the property was subsequently demolished. Premises for the Midland Bank were constructed there in 1912/13, more recently acquired by HSBC Bank. This building has quite a sense of style in its architecture, and is another fine landmark in the street scene, having celebrated its centenary.

Arnison's, 1863 and 2013

The historic photograph most likely dates from 10 March 1863, when the Prince of Wales married Princess Alexandra of Denmark. The decorated arch over Devonshire Street carries the words 'Prince of Wales'. Arnison's ladies' and gentleman's outfitters has overlooked the Market Square for some 270 years, unchanged except for maintenance and new lettering for the name above the frontage. Trading since 1742, Arnison's is the oldest shop in the town with a continuous record.

Arnison's, 2013

The gentleman's shop has its entrance off the 'narrows'; this restricted road later became notorious for causing a bottleneck and traffic jams on what was the main A6 route to and from Scotland before the M6 motorway was opened. The raised lettering of the permanent wall 'posters' was characteristic of Victorian shops, and a historic reminder of an era. Their text, quaint today, harks back to an earlier lifestyle, aiming to serve the sartorial and domestic needs of richer families. The tradition of service continues. The window display has red, white and blue items in celebration of the Queen's Diamond Jubilee.

George Hotel, 1930s and 2013

For many generations, the hotel was owned by the Dukes of Devonshire, eventually being sold at the end of the nineteenth century. The Young Pretender, Charles Edward Stuart, stayed there in 1745 before the last battle on English soil at nearby Clifton Moor. The building fabric has changed little, the only obvious differences being the entrance to the Devonshire Arcade and The Wine House to its right, obscured here by the recently installed display board. Diagonal parking is allowed in the street for a short time. The George is well regarded and something of a social centre; the Penrith Rotary Club and Inner Wheel have their meetings there.

Procession, 1930s, and Olympic Torchbearer, 2012

Nothing brings the populace on to the streets more than a national celebration. The early parade will be a Coronation or Empire Day, whereas the contemporary photograph shows one of the Olympic torchbearers passing the Musgrave monument; the occasion saw the streets through Penrith crowded as for no other event. The torch was preceded and followed by a parade of police and sponsor vehicles, and the excitement and joy of the precursor to Britain's spectacular 2012 Olympic Games was tangible.

Bluebell Bookshop, 1998, and Costa, 2013
A well-known treasure in Penrith, the Bluebell Bookshop offered a huge variety of books on its shelves as well as a large selection of music CDs. It ceased trading quite recently – no doubt a victim of internet book-buying habits. The premises now offer Costa Coffee, harking back to an extent to the role of coffee shops in earlier centuries, when citizens gathered for talk and debate as well as coffee. Angel Square is a pedestrianised development opened in 1988, giving a home to Boots and WHSmith.

Penrith Castle, 1868 and 2012

The castle was begun in 1399, when William Strickland, later Bishop of Carlisle and Archbishop of Canterbury, added a stone curtain wall to the original pele tower. It was improved and added to over the next seventy years, finally to become a royal fortress for Richard, Duke of Gloucester, as 'Guardian of the West March' towards Scotland. Although Governor of Carlisle Castle (later Richard III of England), he often resided in Penrith. Much later, stone from the castle was used for local building, and even a house was located near the walls. The house was removed when the castle and land were transferred from the railway company to the council, and Castle Park created. In the recent photograph, the building on the far right contains recently completed apartments in the Foundry complex.

Castle Park, 1950s and 2012

A busy scene, showing people enjoying themselves in Castle Park, in days when bowls and tennis were more popular than now. The building, which served as a pavilion and provided refreshments, was destroyed by fire. A replacement new building for the same purpose does not attempt the architectural style of the original.

Castletown Railway Bridge, 1850s and 2012
A modern train contrasts with the print from Victorian times when the Lancaster to Carlisle line opened in 1846, bringing benefits in the carriage of goods and export of farm produce. Passenger trains allowed tourism to escalate, with the Lake District as a popular and adventurous destination. The bridge still exists today, carrying the Greystoke Road over the railway line just north of Penrith station, which itself is virtually unchanged since this important rail route was created. The modern train is a direct service to Manchester Airport.

Penrith Railway Station, 1906 and 2012

Visiting the Lakes became very much a popular and adventurous feature of tourism, encouraged by Thomas Cook. The motor charabanc in this early picture had solid tyres and a maximum speed of 12 mph. The majority will be visiting Ullswater, having travelled by train to Penrith from Cheshire and Lancashire or further afield. Today's high-speed trains on the West Coast Main Line between London, Glasgow and Edinburgh carry many business passengers as well as people with other plans. Penrith to London now takes minutes over three hours.

Penrith Railway Station, 1930s and 2012

The station has changed little since the beginning of the twentieth century, the only exception being the construction of a strictly utilitarian two-storey car park for train users. The original station was of a pattern created by the then London, Midland and Scottish Railway; there was a series of designs to cater for different locations and scale of activity. The tallest building was the Stationmaster's House. The 1930s buses all show Ullswater as the destination.

Penrith Railway Station, 1900s, and McDonald's, 2013

In 1900, there were interconnecting trains to Keswick and Cockermouth as well as to the east, seen here on a platform next to the main line. These branch lines were victims of the Beeching cuts. The traditional newspaper kiosk has also disappeared. While not a part of the station, the new McDonald's (*see page 23*) close by is another sign of the times. The periphery has a sandstone wall as a concession to tradition, but the Council did not allow the 26-foot-high yellow 'M' logo for which planning permission was sought.

Steaming Through Penrith, 1950 and 2013

The age of steam is recorded here, with Pacific class 46249 *City of Sheffield* heading north for Carlisle. In contrast, we see a contemporary 'Pendolino' train driven by electricity moving into the station. These so-called 'tilting trains' allow higher speeds on the old track layouts than would otherwise be feasible, thus safely reducing journey times. Most of the drive machinery is below the floor level and the driving experience dramatically different from the steam locomotives of yesteryear. The Alsthom-built 'Pendolino' trains on the West Coast Main Line are capable of 140 mph, but limited to 125 mph through restrictions related to the signalling system.

Fenton House, 1999 and 2013

Fenton House occupies a strategic position in Corney Square near the Town Hall and the north end of Middlegate. For many years it was occupied by Joseph James, a long-standing and traditional furnishing and antiques company, which eventually closed. After refurbishment, the ground floor is occupied by a property company, again emphasising the change of use from goods to services happening universally. The old adjoining single-storey building, once a butcher's shop, at the right has been replaced by new construction, with two storeys above a new shop. This has at least ensured that a pleasing building is retained rather than being demolished.

Threshing Engine, 1900s, and Pressure Vessel in Transit, 1960s

The threshing engine is probably of 1900s vintage, and stands outside Cowper's Chemists former shop in Fenton House and the Clark Butchers shop opposite the Town Hall. One may speculate as to why this major ensemble of agricultural machinery, with its crew of three, was in the town spouting smoke from its boiler. The large pressure vessel in transit, soon to navigate the 'narrows', illustrates the then challenge of the A6 route through the town centre.

Maltster's Arms, 1900s and 2013

There were a disproportionately large number of pubs (up to eighty) in Penrith, many of which have disappeared since the secondary trading in agricultural produce gradually reduced to zero. Wheat, oats, barley and other produce are bought and sold quite differently nowadays. Are the group of children awaiting their father's reappearance after a lunchtime beer, under strict instructions not to move away? Or perhaps hoping to beg a coin from a happy drinker? The Maltster's Arms was in Stricklandgate and is now a private house.

Robinson's School, 1895 and 2013

William Robinson, born in Penrith, became a wealthy London grocer and coffee merchant. On his death in 1670, he endowed a free school for the education of 'poor girls in reading and sempstry' or such other learning as appropriate. The inscription over the door carries his name. Having become a National Infant School, it finally closed as a school in 1971. This Elizabethan building then became the home of the town's Museum and Tourist Information Centre. The accompanying photograph shows the extension which houses the busy Information Centre at the north entrance to Middlegate.

Drill Hall, 1965, and Voreda House, 2013

The Drill Hall in Portland Place was extensively damaged by fire in 1963. Firefighters had to ferry water from the River Eamont as the mains supply was cut off in the very severe winter. The Hall had served as Penrith's social and recreational centre for seventy years, latterly staging hugely popular Saturday night dances as well as hunt balls, marathon jives and beauty contests. The fire-damaged remains were demolished in 1965 to allow the building of Voreda House, now occupied by a component of the NHS. Locals have fought for the retention of the large fir tree.

Coronation Garden, 2008 and 2013

The Coronation Garden in Portland Place behind the Town Hall was inaugurated in 1938 to celebrate the Coronation of George VI in 1937. It had become bare and neglected until a recent initiative by Penrith Rotary Club produced a delightful new addition to the town in the shape of a most attractive and original recreation, stimulated by the centenary celebration of Rotary worldwide. Grants were secured from the Heritage Lottery Fund and Eden District Council, with further assistance from the Rotary Club and sponsors. The original diagonal paths are retained, and a circular path has a timeline set in for the visitor to follow the heritage of Penrith from prehistoric times to the present day. Four artwork sculptures were designed with considerable input from local schools, adding further interest. Removal of a hedge and replacement of railings opens up the garden. Planting includes sensory areas, and there is now a pleasurable attraction for all.

Town Seal, 2013

By the middle of the thirteenth century, Penrith was of sufficient importance to merit its own official seal. The brass seal bears the cross of St Andrew and an inscription which states 'the Common Seal of the Town of Penrith'. It was found some twenty miles away in a churchyard at Brampton, supposedly having been stolen by raiding Scots, and is now safe in Penrith and Eden Museum. The design has appeared in various forms, from the detail of the carving on the Town Hall to this sculpture in the Coronation Garden, and a simplified logo for the New Squares development. (*Copyright of the image of the Medieval Seal belongs to Penrith and Eden Museum [Eden District Council]*)

Musgrave Hall, 1900 and 2012

Originally the home of the Edenhall Musgraves, with family heraldic arms on the lintel, by the late nineteenth century it was owned by Countess Ossalinsky. She owned extensive land at Thirlmere, where Manchester Corporation wanted the lake and surrounding land for development as a reservoir. Having rejected an initial offer, the Countess went to arbitration and was paid considerably more. This corner of Middlegate was peaceful in Victorian times as there was no northern exit. The building now houses the Penrith Branch of the Royal British Legion.

Middlegate, 1930s and 2013

At one time there was a verandah known as the Long Front along the side of Middlegate, much appreciated by customers when the day brought rain. William Jespers & Co. and the neighbouring Ship Hotel were replaced by Burtons store in 1937, when it must have been viewed as a very modern Art Nouveau building. Construction allowed the road to be widened where the former building intruded. Burton's is still there but the verandah has gone.

Alhambra, 2011 and 2013

This rather distinguished row of buildings was built in 1910 on the site of the former Middlegate Brewery. The Alhambra was originally a public assembly hall with a maple floor suitable for then popular roller skating. Middlegate was one of the main streets of old Penrith, becoming 'Medilgate' in 1551. The assembly hall became a multi-screen cinema and bingo hall. The latter was closed, but the cinema gained a new lease of life after strong representation from users supported by the local MP, Rory Stewart. The bingo hall is now a restaurant called the Indian Plaza.

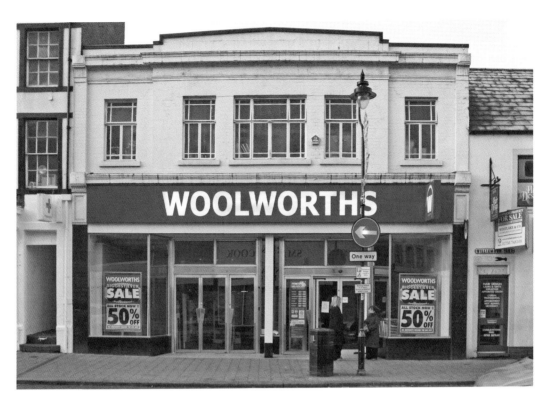

Woolworths, 2010, and B&M Bargains, 2013

Woolworths, with its rather grand frontage, much to everyone's surprise, ceased trading with discounts on all the contents of the store. Very soon B&M Bargains was installed, bringing more change to one side of Middlegate and pursuing a business model very like Woolworths when it advertised goods for 3d and 6d, now at prices reflecting inflation since those days.

Portland Place, 1900 and 2013

The 1900 photograph is at the junction with Wilson Row and has the former Christ Church Rooms, now the Masonic Hall, at the corner with the lamp standard. Wordsworth House would then have been opposite, later to become the Town Hall. The Victorian houses are quite large and spacious, suitable for adaptation to B&Bs or guest houses as the demand for hotels lessened. This trend was mainly a result of motor car use for both business and private purposes. The old streets necessarily filled with roadside parking, as the houses had little space for cars. The provision here north of the town centre was complemented by a line of guest houses to the south in Victoria Road.

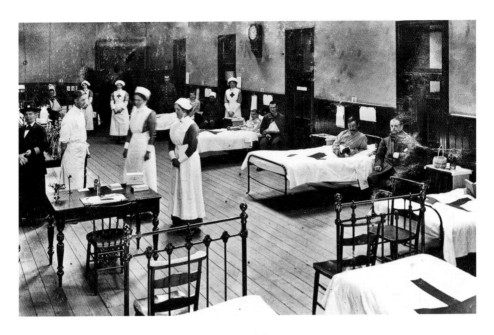

Auxiliary Hospital, 1914–18, and War Memorial, 1920s

Although the photograph is slightly damaged, it clearly conveys the formality and discipline of those days. It is believed that the ward is in what originally was Christ Church Rooms, and the Auxiliary Hospital was set up in three separate Penrith locations managed as one unit. Lest we forget, the Penrith War Memorial at the entrance to Castle Park reminds us of that terrible world event.

Penrith Methodist Church, 1904 and 2012

The church is a fine Victorian building, constructed in 1873 for £8,000 when the earlier chapel built in Fell Lane in 1813 became too small. The church was enhanced internally, and a new foyer added in 1997 for more than a hundred times as much. In addition to regular church activities, the meeting rooms and church itself are used for a variety of events, notably for musical performances; there is even a concert-quality Steinway grand piano. As with all buildings from the era, there is limited provision for car parking.

Crozier Lodge, 1865 and 2012

Then at the head of Sandgate before streets were constructed rising up the Beacon Hill, the house was built in 1826 by William Harrison, a Penrith gunsmith, and named after his wife Ann Crozier. By the 1850s, the Reverend William Brewis was the tenant, whose two daughters, the Misses Brewis, ran a girls' school there until 1879. One was the headmistress, and the teachers are here seen in the garden talking to the top-hatted gardener. Weekly boarding was charged at twenty guineas per annum. Samuel Plimsoll, a Penrith resident famous for the Plimsoll Line used on ships to gauge the loading, was reputedly a visitor. Today the house remains a private property.

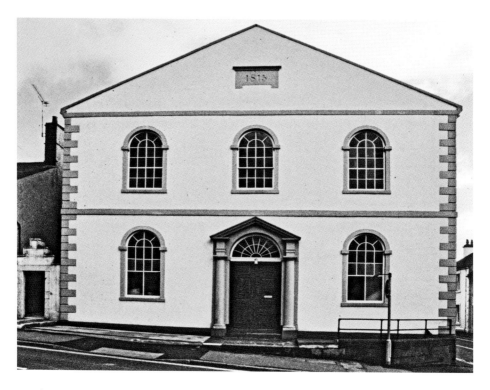

Sandgate Head Chapel, 1998 and 2013

The church was built by the Wesleyans and has an 1813 date stone. It was purchased by the Primitive Methodists in 1873, when the Wesleyans moved to their fine new church in Wordsworth Street. In its time, the Fell Lane building was described as a most comfortable place of worship. Inside, it was fitted with pitch-pine seats for 550, and had a beautifully designed rostrum. In the rear, there was a lecture hall, minister's vestry, classrooms and an adjoining cottage. Sadly, it has been unused for years, although there were plans for conversion to apartments, and in 2013 the building looks rather sorry.

Scott's Fish Restaurant, 2000, and Foundry 34, 2011

Scott's was a popular take-away fish and chip shop coupled with a restaurant in Sandgate, based on a much earlier house. More recently, it became Foundry 34 (the name referring to Altham's foundry which was located there and made cast iron stoves and other products), still maintaining the fish and chip outlet and restaurant, but extending the building upwards and rearwards to create the present hotel – certainly an imaginative use of space. The restaurant has moved up-market to become quite sophisticated.

Co-op, 1930 and 2012

Having been founded in 1890, the large store in Burrowgate with a 1931 date stone has changed little in appearance over the years. Unusually, it has retained its independence, acquiring other co-ops in the region. The Penrith store was extensively refurbished in 2008; the food store became Food@19 (19 Burrowgate). The Somerfield supermarket became 'The Co-operative Food', which has a strong ethical tradition, for example supporting Fair Trade. From the company's foundation there was free delivery for customers' purchases, of great value to elderly and less mobile people.

St Andrew's Boys School, 1982, and Hutton Court, 2013

The Boys School in Benson Row was deemed to have completed its useful life and was demolished. The school was founded in 1816, rebuilt in 1870 and closed in 1979. In its place was built a new block of flats of undistinguished design. Over the Hutton Court name there is an inset memento of the past. 'Bulldogs' refers to the practice of keeping dogs for bull-baiting, supposed to improve the quality of beef before the beast was slaughtered in the nearby shambles. Abattoirs and records of meat traceability have changed since those days. No doubt the boys enjoyed being called and emulating bulldogs.

Regent Cinema, 1983 and 2013

The former cinema has become the Eden Rural Foyer, a centre for skills learning, now with nearby accommodation extended very considerably by new building, recently completed. It is a community resource by Impact Housing for young people to access training and equip themselves for employment.

Friargate, 2011 and 2013
Almost the last of the motor car agents actually in Penrith town, the C. G. Ford building has been demolished to make way for new apartments, reflecting the design and style of the adjacent street scene. The roadside parked car population has increased, but the overall impression has greater coherence. The emerging Friargate, including work in progress at Hutton Hall and Mostyn Hall (former Greggs bakery sites), may well be an attractive addition to the town.

Hutton Hall, 1982 and 2013

A Grade II* English Heritage listed building in Friargate with a pele tower, the hall belonged to the family whose name it bears, probably living here as early as the reign of Edward I. Hutton Hall remained in their possession until 1734, and was later sold to the Earl of Lonsdale. The principal steward on the Lowther Estate lived there for a period. Birketts the Bakers used the hall as offices, and various ugly buildings behind and along Benson Row to produce their wares, as did Greggs when they acquired Birketts. Greggs, in time, moved to a custom-designed state-of-the-art factory on the Trading Estate, seen here under a threatening sky. McCarthy and Stone plan retirement apartments on the former site, and clearance of the industrial buildings is taking place. One trusts that the hall and pele tower, with its roof visible behind the adjacent cottage, will find a sympathetic future.

Sandgate, 1950s, and Bus Station, 2013

The busy scene results from the Sandgate stop-over for long distance coaches. The Royston Snack Bar was popular for drivers and travellers. While coach traffic may have lessened with the opening of the M6 motorway, the bus station remains busy and there is a large adjacent car park. The new bus station involved some demolition of buildings in Sandgate to allow for a one-way system for vehicles to enter and leave. The entrance is shown here.

Wordsworth Street, *c.* 1900 and 2013

As one of the 'New Streets', Worthsworth Street looks down into a much less developed town, contrasting with the view in 2013 with many parked cars down the hill and much building beyond. Happily, the Victorian houses survive, as do the sandstone garden walls, and the only negative thoughts are in the minds of drivers, with obstacles either side.

Cottage Hospital and Jubilee Lodge, 2012

The Jubilee Cottage Hospital on Beacon Edge was erected by public subscription in 1898 and later enlarged. It was located on Beacon Edge adjacent to the cemetery, the site having been donated by the Earl of Lonsdale. Management passed from Penrith to the NHS in 1948 and the hospital finally closed in 1985, having served Penrith for almost a century, patients and staff moving to a new purpose-built hospital on Bridge Lane where there is a Jubilee Ward among enlarged facilities and services. The Cottage Hospital was refurbished as Jubilee Lodge, containing nine apartments. The new owners were provided with garages for their cars.

Caroline Cottage, 1900s and 2012

Built in 1818, the Keeper's Lodge was named after the 1st Earl of Lonsdale's youngest daughter. A path close by gave access to the Beacon Fell. In former years, visitors signed a book in the porch (the path is 'Permissive' rather than 'Public'). Today, access is by a path further west along the Beacon Edge road, offering a gently sloping climb up to the Beacon, popular with dogs and their owners. At the top, 286 metres above sea level, it is possible to see Ullswater, Scottish mountains across the Solway Firth, Blencathra, Lake District fells peak after peak, and the Pennines.

Beacon Monument, *c.* 1905 and 2013

At the top of the Beacon Hill is the Beacon monument of 1719, 400 feet above the town and constructed of local sandstone, the site from which a beacon would have been fired to signal a Napoleonic invasion or threats from the north. The 1905 photograph shows the monument at a time when the Beacon Hill was less tree-covered. The beacons (the first recorded in 1296) were simply bonfires of wood and branches, replaced later by pitch-boxes. It is listed in 1468, communicating with one at Dale Raughton on high ground above Kirkoswald and Carlisle Castle high tower beacon. Southwards, it could be seen from Orton Scar.

Cornmarket, 1930s and 2013

A busy street scene in Cornmarket, with the Musgrave monument and St Andrew's church tower in the distance, shows several motor cars and a horse and cart. There was an underground public toilet, as were usual some decades ago. The Market Cross has been introduced, which can house market stalls or, on occasion, the Penrith Town Band. Whereas the basic buildings are very little changed the street-level businesses are very different.

Poet's Walk, 2013

The Fish Hotel, as Cornmarket joins Castlegate, offered food, drink and accommodation for many years, but was demolished in 1972 to allow the building of Poet's Walk which offers a range of shops with pedestrian access. Portraits of Wordsworth and Coleridge appear over the entrance, and a variety of businesses have traded over the years in this shopping precinct.

Market Cross, 1984 and 2013

Earlier views of Cornmarket show a different configuration at the junction with Great Dockray. A rather impressive horse trough located near this point was relocated in Castle Park and this new structure named the Market Cross was designed and erected in 1984. It could be used for shelter of market stalls and their customers, offering a social gathering place. It could also house the Penrith Town Band or other performers.

Gloucester Arms Hotel, 1900s and 2012

The hotel has also been known as Dockray Hall and is Penrith's only Grade I English Heritage listed building. A plaque on the front of the building claims that it was 'traditionally the residence of Richard, Duke of Gloucester, afterwards Richard III'. The Duke's arms are prominently displayed over the entrance. Over another doorway we see 'JW 1580'; the initials are of John de Whelpdale who remodelled the hall. Mythology avows that there is an underground passage between Penrith Castle and the kitchens, presumably for the Duke of Gloucester's convenience. No evidence has been found.

Tuesday Market, 2000 and 2011

Even in the millennium year, the Tuesday market was flourishing but, more recently, the area has only a small residual sales activity (here under the Market Cross) and the remainder of Great Dockray is again full of parked cars. There has been an initiative to establish a monthly farmer's market in Market Square, but that has attracted only a few offering farm-produced foods (*see page 13*). Thus, with these trends and the earlier move of the auction mart, the 'historic market town' is transformed to 'supermarket town'.

Penrith Main Post Office, 1955 and 2013

The main post and sorting office in Crown Square acquired an updated appearance compared with the 1955 version. Delivery vans are parked in a yard reached by the covered entrance, emerging in the early morning for circuits around local villages accessed via Penrith. The white building is newly built as part of the New Squares scheme, further along the road abutting the Sykes fishing gear shop (Grade II English Heritage listed) as the only shop retained after the Sunlight laundry was demolished.

Penrith Auction Mart, 1950s, and Agricultural Hotel, 2013

An auction mart was established in 1870, in time outgrowing the original site. When the area was vacated it allowed a new supermarket for Safeway (later Morrisons) to be built, accessed from Brunswick Road, and for the Penrith Players Theatre to be housed. The mart was re-established at Skirsgill on the west side of the M6 near junction 40. The mart was operated by Penrith Farmers and Kidd's and opened in 1987, dealing not only with cattle but also furniture, art, household and business items. The day-to-day agricultural operation was assumed by Penrith & District Farmers Mart in 2002. Close by the early mart is the Agricultural Hotel, popular with the farming community.

Old Pens and Skirsgill Auction Mart, *c.* 1950 and 2013
Here the pens are well occupied by sheep about to be auctioned having been delivered by vehicle,
and we see the extensive building complex of the new Skirsgill Mart with farmers' vehicles on
a sale day for sheep.

Old and Skirsgill Mart Ring, *c.* 1950 and 2013
A nostalgic view inside the old mart contrasts with the new sale ring, where the auctioneer is in full flow with a consignment of sheep.

Morrisons Fire, 2009

In December 2009, Morrisons suffered a major outbreak of fire that started in the pharmacy, severely damaging the store and contents. Fortunately, no one was injured. The morning after the fire, a fire engine was still standing by. The company lost no time in deciding on a recovery plan, resulting in improved facilities.

Morrisons, 2010

Within a remarkably short time, there was an air-conditioned tented building over part of the parking area and new steelwork in place for extensions to the original Safeway supermarket. The tented store offered a more limited range of produce, but was appreciated by Morrisons customers. The 'new' store gained from Morrisons' operational experience and was fully in business again less than a year after the fire, a tribute to the efforts of management, staff and contractors. The reconfigured store, early on a Sunday morning in August 2010, has the new main entrance beneath the name and clock. Warehousing is to the right, where old buildings nearby were demolished to make way for the new.

Ribble Garage, 1930s and 1992
Buses manufactured in the 1920s are seen at the Ribble Garage in Brunswick Road, with staff lined up in the foreground. As well as regular local services, journeys in well-appointed coaches to far destinations were popular and less expensive than rail. Comfort stops were necessary, and the wide space of Sandgate attracted the operators and their passengers (*see page 49*). The Brunswick Road Garage, for sale much later, looks forlorn.

Bowmans and Rickerby's, 2010

Booths, the northern supermarket group, had targeted Penrith as their choice of location for a new store, acquiring Bowman's (who had made a valiant attempt to re-use the former bus garage) and Rickerby's next door to each other on Brunswick Road. Both were demolished to make space for the new store and associated car parking. Rickerby's reappeared with a new green logo on the Trading Estate and its business of selling and supporting agricultural machinery much in evidence.

Booths, 2011

Following demolition of the Bowman and Rickerby buildings and site clearance, steelwork emerged from the mists of January 2011. Careful preparation and pre-planning, supported by a well-organised work force, led to the appearance by September of a recognisable building. Although of contemporary appearance, it clearly was sympathetic to the traditional architecture of the town, not solely because of the use of sandstone cladding. The two gables at the left became the frontage of a separate business offering outdoor and sports clothing.

Booths Opening, November 2011 and 2013

When the Booths Brunswick Road store opened on 15 November 2011, it was evidently going to be a somewhat stylish event presided over by Edwin Booth himself. Penrith Town Band provided the music, and the horse-drawn delivery dray and a carriage were present for the occasion. On the previous evening, many local people had been invited to view the store. This inspection was well attended and hosted, and it was clear that a great deal of thought had been devoted to the store's internal layout and furnishings to support the enticing range of produce on offer. Externally, the completed store looks well.

Brunswick Road School, 1900s and 2013

Brunswick Road School has traditional buildings and demonstrates little change in more than a century, apart from looking rather more cheerful in the sunshine. Children enter and exit the school from the other side (the Bluebell Car Park) rather than from the busy Brunswick Road. No doubt, the age of the buildings is compensated for by enthusiastic staff and pupils.

The Castle, 2010 and 2013

Castletown is the area of the town lying to the west of the railway line, where The Castle was the only remaining public house. Looking more and more neglected, the builders moved in and this seemed to signal the demise of another pub. But it was not demolished, and there emerged a smart row of living accommodation to grace Norfolk Road after refurbishment of these older buildings.

King Street, 1900 and 2013

At the turn of the century, the street is full of delivery carts, hand and horse-drawn, and quite a number of people. St Andrew's church tower is visible. In 2013, we see the imposing building of Lloyds Bank and the Penrith Building Society, the latter having a major role in creating the Victorian 'new streets'. On a Sunday morning there are few cars in evidence, unlike during weekdays.

Cumberland and Westmorland Herald, 1950s and 2013

The popular local paper, with a readership of some 40,000 people, had its printing works in King Street, and we see a Bowaters vehicle and trailer delivering newsprint. The *Herald* joined the digital revolution and now functions in a modern office, formerly Armstrong and Fleming Garage in King Street. Using digital technology has allowed the introduction of colour printing and many pages now have colour, especially welcomed by those advertising in the paper.

Cowper's Chemists, c. 1900 and 2013

Cowper's at one time had a second establishment in Fenton House near the Town Hall. From 50 King Street, the business has extended southwards, while the Cockbrayne building became the Robin Hood Inn frontage, originally entered from Rowcliffe Lane which runs parallel with King Street. Many appreciate the independence, personal service, traditional mahogany shop furniture and convenience of this centrally-located shop. The Robin Hood Inn next door is famous for a stay by William Wordsworth and his friend Raisley Calvert, who was unwell and died some months later. He left Wordsworth a handsome legacy of £900, thus fostering his life as a poet rather than entering a profession as his family wished.

Crown Hotel, 1928, and Supermarket, 2013

The Crown Hotel was famous in its era and offered coach and charabanc trips to Ullswater and other beauty spots for its customers. It later became the Royal Hussar and was eventually demolished to allow the building of a supermarket, latterly trading as Somerfield but now carrying The Co-operative Food sign. The pizza outlet joins a number of restaurants on the east side of King Street.

Victoria Road, 1910 and 2012

Leading via King Street from Market Square to the south and Kemplay roundabout, this thoroughfare was once a route for horse-drawn farm carts and is now busy with cars and other vehicles. A conclave of B&B establishments caters for visitors, and there is John Norris, a famous store for those interested in the sport of fishing. There is a variety of other businesses as well as residential properties. The New Squares development has required a new junction at the visible traffic lights, where Kilgour Street joins.

Beacon Garage, 1930s

At the Beacon Garage, the car leading the fine display is offered for £150, a far cry from even the lowest-priced vehicles today. The hanging sign above the garage describes 'Keiser's Garage', referring presumably to the owner, a German who stayed behind during the Kaiser's visit before the Great War to act as chauffeur for the Earl of Lonsdale. The interior of this workshop in Southend Road is very different from the servicing bay of a modern garage. Here there are no less than six technicians busy with machinery, whereas today there would be a diagnostic laptop and online ordering of replacement parts with the faulty unit discarded. Note belt-driven lathes would not be permitted nowadays for safety reasons.

Walton's Garage, 2010 and 2013

Walton's Garage sell Toyotas, economical Japanese cars from one of the long-established firms in that country, and it was necessary that their considerable space was released for the New Squares scheme. They moved from Southend Road to the industrial estate where several motor car agents have established themselves, compared with the historic times when the pioneers traded in King Street, Victoria Road and Southend Road. The industrial estate allows more space for showrooms, workshops and cars on display outside for the benefit of customers.

Victoria Road, 1900 and 2013

Looking along Victoria Road towards the town centre, these rather stylish Victorian houses proved readily adaptable to become B&Bs or guest houses, complementing those in Portland Place to the north of the town centre. With no garages, there is roadside parking along their frontage, although a number have space at the rear accessed from Southend Road. The convenient location is only a few minutes' walk to the centre of the town. The front railings were lost through the metal-collecting frenzy of the Second World War. While they compete with each other, no doubt there is cooperation when a potential guest might not secure a bed for the night.

Victoria Road New Apartments, 2009 and 2011

The scale of construction is well illustrated in the earlier view. These apartments emerged on some scale, absorbing the site of the former RAFA Club to form the entrance to the new Kilgour Street. Many locals wonder where the people are coming from to occupy all this accommodation, and especially where they will keep their cars. They cannot all be pedestrians, despite living so close to the town centre!

Cottage Hospital, *c.* 1900, and Penrith Hospital, 2013

The Victorian Cottage Hospital, with a nurse at the window, contrasts with the busy scene at Penrith and Eden Community Hospital today, where the range of activity and services are greatly extended from those days. Consultants from Cumberland Infirmary and other hospitals operate a wide range of day clinics; there are normally no long-stay patients and there is a range of ancillary medical services. The League of Friends provides up-to-date equipment for many of these services. An assessment centre deals with urgent needs by routing patients to appropriate medical services. Doctors from the health centre practices undertake emergencies, for example attending road traffic accidents using fully-equipped vehicles, and there is good communication with Mountain Rescue and Air Ambulance.

B&Q, 2009 and 2013

B&Q has operated at its then new building in Bridge Lane since 1989. New buildings have been erected at the Davidson's truck stop on Ullswater Road. Neighbouring land already has Aldi and Halfords, and the whole area will become a dominant edge-of-town retail park with five new retail units totalling 61,000 square feet, of which a new store for B&Q will form the largest component. The substantial construction is shown, with the further section for B&Q, although the other new occupants are not evident. The current B&Q building will house another firm.

Cranston's, 1914 and 2013

Cranston's Master Butchers was established in 1914 by the current directors' great uncle, Stanley Cranston, who developed a reputation for selling top quality meat products in the Eden Valley from his horse and cart. Cranston's now operate four traditional butcher's shops and the flagship Cumbrian Food Hall. The site also includes facilities for packing and processing, serving a busy catering and wholesale business. The more recent Café Oswalds is popular with locals and visitors alike. Cranston's Master Butchers source locally, direct from farmers and producers, to offer wholesome and delicious foods which have won many awards nationally. The photograph of the Food Hall and Café was taken on Easter Sunday when the business was closed and there were no customers' cars parked.

Fire Station, 2012 and 2013

A new community fire station is operational, located on a greenfield site at Kemplay Roundabout adjacent to Carleton Hall, the headquarters of Cumbria Constabulary. Carleton Hall buildings are seen to the left. The fire service has expanded in size and scope over the years, often having a role in almost any emergency. The roundabout traffic flow is controlled by lights so that emergency vehicles can quickly exit. The building also houses other County Council functions and will facilitate this vital service.

McDonalds and Kentucky Fried Chicken, 2012

Fast-food outlets join the scene everywhere and, since the millennium year, both McDonalds and Kentucky Fried Chicken have built on previously unused sites, the former near the railway station (*see page 23*) and the latter near the Kemplay Roundabout at the A66/A6 junction on the southern edge of the town. Both buildings are of a design to match outlets elsewhere, although their sites are enclosed with traditional sandstone walls and served by quite large car parking areas.

Creating the New Squares Site, 2008

As a reminder, we have the Southend Road car park and the Penrith Football Club site. The origin of the New Squares scheme dates back into the 1990s when Eden District Council decided the town should have another supermarket, the Southend Road car park acting as a basis. It became clear that Penrith Football Club would have to move elsewhere. With various demolitions, including Walton's Garage, the Sunlight Laundry, the Football Club buildings, and many other smaller areas, a very substantial tract was freed. Temporary traffic lights and road closures have caused a nuisance for traffic flow over a five-year period. Final details are due for completion mid-year 2013.

Penrith Football Club, 2008 and 2013
The football match illustrated is possibly the last on the historical site in Penrith. The new stand and football field is undoubtedly a great improvement and will generate its own traditions (and hopefully successes) as the local club sustains its future.

Work Begins, 2008

The scheme finally began in earnest in mid-2008 when machines moved in to break up the tarmac surfacing of Southend Road car park. Site preparation in other areas was also in progress. Eden District Council had appointed a local developer to lead the project, and detailed plans had been exhibited to the public as part of the consultation process. At first, rapid progress was made, but activity suddenly stopped as the bank behind the £90 million scheme withdrew funding in the aftermath of the global financial crisis. A consequence was that the developer was forced into administration, and the site left untouched much to the alarm of townspeople.

~Eden

Please be advised that Thomas Armstrong Ltd will commence work on the carpark for the Penrith New Squares Development as from Monday 9th June 2008

New Squares Development, 2008–13

The discarded hard hat above symbolises frustration associated with the New Squares funding fiasco, albeit caused by remote events. However, Sainsbury's stepped in and activity once again accelerated towards satisfactory delivery of the scheme. A condition was that the supermarket itself should be completed first, with retail units for separate occupancy to follow. Below, we see a plan for the overall New Squares scheme. The orange areas designate the 93,000 square feet of retail space, and the 700 new car parking spaces are shown. The Common Garden Square is intended as a public open space where events can be held. Pedestrian access to the town centre is through Two Lions Square and Princes Square.

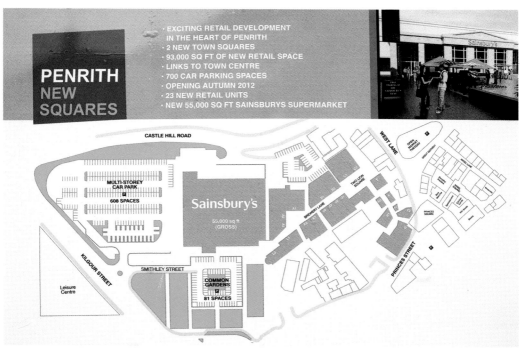

PENRITH NEW SQUARES

- EXCITING RETAIL DEVELOPMENT IN THE HEART OF PENRITH
- 2 NEW TOWN SQUARES
- 93,000 SQ FT OF NEW RETAIL SPACE
- LINKS TO TOWN CENTRE
- 700 CAR PARKING SPACES
- OPENING AUTUMN 2012
- 23 NEW RETAIL UNITS
- NEW 55,000 SQ FT SAINSBURYS SUPERMARKET

Sainsbury's Opening, 2011

At the opening of Sainsbury's in November 2011, visitors were parked in Common Garden Square and part of the remaining development is shielded from view. A school choir in the store ensured the mothers were present. There have been questions as to whether the 'classical' frontage of Sainsbury's is in keeping with the town's architectural style, but it can be argued that the environment in what was a rather ugly part of the town has been vastly improved. A supermarket is basically a large shed with a frontage, after all!

Kilgour Street, 2013
The scheme demanded a new road, Kilgour Street (named after Dr Kilgour, a well-known Penrith doctor of Scots origin), running from Victoria Road to Castle Hill Drive and the access for deliveries to Sainsbury's. Laying of part of the street is illustrated, and the street soon gathered a selection of signage and will eventually appear on the town map. Although shown, the provision of parking for buses and coaches is very limited.

Common Garden and Castle Hill Drive Housing, 2013
Looking from Sainsbury's, we see part of the Common Garden Square with new housing beyond. In the reverse direction, there are new apartments on Castle Hill Drive, all in the same general style of architecture. However, there are features of the building configuration – colour finish, roof detailing, plan shapes and so on – which introduce pleasing variety to an extent not normally evident in housing estates.

Tun House and Route to Town Centre, 2013
Just beside the Sainsbury's frontage is now an ironwork archway which signals the route to Penrith town centre through Brewery Lane to Two Lions Square, and Bowling Green Lane to Princes Square. At this location there is Tun House, a building of some architectural interest fronting the iconic three-storey buildings that predominate. It certainly has a good view of Sainsbury's as well as Common Garden Square. There remained a barrier to the flow of pedestrians.

Princes Square and New Squares Entrance, 2013

The New Squares development is linked with the town centre through Princes Square and Two Lions Square. The latter is named after the Two Lions building, formerly the town house of Gerard Lowther and for many years a disused Whitbread pub. It is English Heritage listed and contains a unique plasterwork ceiling of some merit. The entry for pedestrians is designated by the ironwork arch at Bowling Green Lane.

Sainsbury's and the New Squares Development, 2013
The store is fully operational and will benefit, in terms of shoppers, from the occupation of all the new housing as part of the New Squares scheme, as well as extensive house-building imminent on greenfield areas to the south-east of the town centre. The population is increasing, and should welcome the very considerable increase in retail outlets now in the town. Changes in use of the small shops in the town centre will perhaps be regretted, with many fondly remembered and some new businesses not generally popular. But this is progress, mirroring what is happening in many small market towns everywhere.

SY *Lady of the Lake*, c. 1900 and 2013

The Steam Yacht *Lady of the Lake* offered a sightseeing sail on Ullswater (*see pages 23 and 24*), which was very popular and considered by many to be the most beautiful of the lakes. In the early 1900s we see the steam-powered *Lady* as she was launched in 1877. She is now the oldest passenger-carrying boat in the world in regular service. With the *Raven*, a larger vessel launched in 1889, both boats were re-engined with Cummins diesels in the mid-1930s. Passengers would disembark at the Pooley Bridge pier, climbing aboard the coach en route to the station, George Hotel or the Crown Hotel. The Ullswater Steam Navigation Company, founded in 1859, continues to ply the lake between Glenridding, Howtown and Pooley Bridge as a prime visitor attraction. Winter timetables and other events are operated by three smaller boats: the *Lady Dorothy*, the *Lady Wakefield*, and the *Western Belle*, classics of their kind.

Lowther Castle, 1910 and 2012

The Lowther family has been associated with Penrith region for centuries; forebear of the Earls of Lonsdale, Gerard Lowther, had a town house in Penrith. The 5th Earl of Lonsdale was known as the 'Yellow Earl' from his yellow racing colours. He was the first president of the Automobile Association, which adopted the yellow colour for all their vehicles. In boxing there is the 'Lonsdale Belt'. Beside sports, the Earl of Lonsdale was a motor car enthusiast and owned a large number, eleven vehicles, mainly Napiers, here lined up with their chauffeurs in front of Lowther Castle. He and the Countess led a high life, and there was a famous visit by the Kaiser and his entourage before the Great War. The family riches came at least partly from investment in West Cumbria, where Whitehaven was at one time the third largest port in Britain. When the 5th Earl died in 1944, the family sold the contents of the castle and removed the roof to pay death duties and avoid local taxes. Recently, the castle is being refurbished, partly with European Community funds, in stages to act as a conference centre and visitor attraction. Here we see the rear of the castle showing something of the scale of refurbishment. The extensive gardens are also being renovated; visitors are welcome and are invited to contribute to the work of the new Trust which manages the venture.